DESERT
WARPAINT

DESERT
WARPAINT

PETER R MARCH

OSPREY
AEROSPACE

Acknowledgements

This unique album of photographs depicting coalition aircraft involved in Operations *Desert Shield* and *Desert Storm* would not have been possible without the generous help given by the photographers whose names appear in the captions. In particular Randy Jolly and David F Brown for the provision of the US aircraft photographs and Squadron Leader Mike Rondot (RAF Jaguar pilot based at Muharraq), Air Vice Marshal Ian Macfadyen, Chief of Staff, HQ BFME, Riyadh, during the conflict and subsequently Commander in Chief BFME, and Yves Debay, Ian Black and Duncan Cubitt for their varied contributions. Assistance with caption information came from Patrick Allen, Bob Archer, Roy Braybrook, Tony Holmes, Paul Jackson, Lindsay Peacock and Tim Ripley, to whom I am most grateful.

Published in 1992 by Osprey Publishing Limited
59 Grosvenor Street, London W1X 9DA

© Osprey Publishing

ISBN 1 85532 1939

Editor Tony Holmes
Page design by Paul Kime
Printed in Hong Kong

Front cover Painted up to celebrate the squadron's remarkable performance during *Desert Storm* operations, A-7E Corsair (BuNo 160552), call sign 'Decoy 400', of VA-72 'Bluehawks' was photographed soon after returning ashore to its NAS Cecil Field, Florida, home base. Allocated to CVW-3's Commander Air Group (CAG), this machine received its one-off scheme on the cruise back from the Gulf aboard USS *John F Kennedy* (CV-67). VA-72 dropped more than one million pounds of ordnance during 362 combat sorties in the Gulf, its pilots totalling over 1500 hours of stick time (*David F Brown*)

Back cover Armed with a pair of suitably inscribed GBU-10 Paveway II 2000 lb laser guided bombs, an F-15E Strike Eagle from the 335th Tactical Fighter Squadron (TFS)/4th Tactical Wing sits on the ramp at Al Kharji, Saudi Arabia, awaiting the arrival of its crew. As can be clearly seen, the USAF made no attempt to obscure the unit markings worn in peacetime by its frontline squadrons, unlike the RAF (*Randy Jolly*)

Title page A dual role F-15E Strike Eagle is seen here with cluster bombs loaded ready for action at Al Kharji, Saudi Arabia. As with most USAF aircraft it retained its normal paint scheme after deployment from Seymour Johnson, North Carolina, in August 1990, initially to Thumrait, Oman. The 4th TFW(P) operated 48 F-15Es (335th and 336th TFS) along with F-15C Eagles (53rd TFS) and F-16A/B Fighting Falcons (138th TFS and 157th TFS) for combined operations (*Randy Jolly*)

For a catalogue of all books published by Osprey Aerospace please write to:

**The Marketing Department,
Octopus Illustrated Books, 1st Floor, Michelin House,
81 Fulham Road, London SW3 6RB**

RAF Jaguars from Nos 6, 41 and 54 Squadrons at Coltishall were initially deployed to Thumrait in August, moving north to Bahrain in October. They were painted overall in RAF desert pink before flying out, and all squadron identities were obliterated. Small code letters were carried on the aircraft fin and the serial in the usual place on the fuselage. By the time that they returned to the UK, as seen here, most Jaguars carried colourful nose art on the port side, together with mission markings below the cockpit *(Bob Archer)*

Introduction

On 2 August 1990 Iraq invaded its tiny neighbour Kuwait, rapidly moving south to the border of Saudi Arabia. Kuwait's small air force, equipped with a handful of A-4KU Skyhawks, BAe Hawk Mk 64s and Mirage F.ICKs was no match for over 800 Iraqi combat aircraft, and its formidable army.

Although the majority of the United Nations condemned the invasion when it appeared that Iraq might continue to march into Saudi Arabia, Saddam Hussein, Iraq's President, was seemingly unmoved by UN Resolutions including No 661 on 6 August that imposed economic sanctions. On the following day, 7 August, President Bush announced that US fighter aircraft were to be sent to Saudi Arabia. Thus began the huge deployment of men and machines on a scale never seen before. Almost all US frontline types (except the B-1B Lancer) were to see service first in the build up – Operation *Desert Shield* – and then in the air war – Operation *Desert Storm*. The RAF was quick to respond also, sending a combined squadron of Tornado F.3s on Armament Practice Camp (APC) at Akrotiri to Dhahran, together with Jaguar GR.1As and Tornado GR.1s to Bahrain before the end of August under the code name Operation *Granby*. The French, Italians and Canadians were all quickly involved with deployments of frontline aircraft. At sea there was a correspondingly big multi-national build up of surface vessels, including US Navy aircraft carriers.

By 17 January 1991 the stage was set for the most effective use of air power the world has ever seen. Led by the Americans, the coalition aircraft effectively destroyed the Iraqi Air Force and key elements of the country's infrastructure in just a few weeks. From the time that absolute air supremacy had been achieved by the coalition air arms, the removal of Iraqi forces from Kuwait was inevitable. On 24 February the ground war, Operation *Desert Sabre*, began. The Iraqi Army had been 'steered' into the belief that the attack would come from the sea. This was not to be as the main thrust was from the south-west and west, with pincer movement cutting the Iraqi forces off from their supply lines to the north. President Bush announced a ceasefire at midnight on 27 February and on 3 March it was formally signed. The Gulf War was over.

Many types of aircraft and weapons saw operational service for the first time in *Desert Storm*. 'Newcomers' like the F-117A, F-15E Strike Eagle and Tornado took their place alongside veterans such as the B-52G, F-4 Phantom II and A-7 Corsair II. New tactics were employed, most, but not all of which were successful. The use of the E-3 AWACS as an airborne radar command and control system was notable, as was the precision laser guided bombing by several types of aircraft and the effective use of radar suppression missiles.

This *Desert Warpaint* book takes a look at the wide range of aircraft operated in the Gulf during *Desert Storm*, and the colourful warpaint that some of them employed. It does not set out to be comprehensive nor all-embracing, but rather more it aims to give a representative picture of the diverse and interesting aircraft, and their markings, operated by the coalition air arms during the Gulf War. *Desert Warpaint* is a personal collation of photographs showing these aircraft and their colour schemes and individual markings.

Peter R March
October 1991

Right Air-to-air refuelling resources were provided by most of the participating air arms, not least the US Marine Corps. Retaining its light grey colour scheme this KC-130T Hercules was based at Bahrain, and hailed from VMGR-152, normally based at Marine Corps Air Station (MCAS) Futenma, Okinawa *(Yves Debay)*

Contents

USAF and USAFE

Left and overleaf A total of 249 F-16 Fighting Falcons were deployed to the USAF's CENTCOM in the Gulf for fighter-bomber duties. They retained their normal paint schemes and unit markings. These F-16Cs with the base code MY came from the 69th TFS/347th TFW at Moody AFB, Georgia and operated with the 388th TPW(P) at Al Minhad, United Arab Emirates, from October 1990. They carried Sidewinder missiles on the wingtips for self-defence, underwing ECM jamming pods, fuel tanks, and cluster bombs on the centreline pylons *(Randy Jolly)*

Above During the early hours of 17 January 1991 the first strike against key Iraqi communications centres was made by 24 Lockheed F-117As operating from Khamis Mushayt, Saudi Arabia. A total of 42 F-117s was deployed from the 37th TFW at Tonopah, Nevada. The 415th TFS flew from its home base to Langley, Virginia, and on 20 August directly to Saudi Arabia with air-to-air refuelling from KC-10A Extenders. As seen here on aircraft 832, they retained their all over 'stealthy' black paint scheme *(Ian Macfadyen)*

Left Nose art and mission markings were carried by many of the F-16 Fighting Falcons on their return from the Gulf. This F-16C from the 10th TFS/50th TFW at Hahn AB, Germany, was decorated with a knight in shining armour as *Sabre One*. It was one of 24 aircraft that deployed from Hahn to Al Dhafra, Sharjah, in November 1990 to form part of the 363rd TFW(P), along with 44 aircraft of the 17th and 33rd TFSs from Shaw AFB, South Carolina *(Tony Holmes)*

Above Most of the F-117s carried a tally of missions on the port side of the nose below the cockpit, and 'theatre art' on the inside of the nose wheel and bomb doors. 'Spell Bound' was one such emblem photographed on an F-117 in Saudi Arabia shortly after the air war ceased *(Ian Macfadyen)*

Left The partly underground hardened aircraft shelters at Khamis Mushayt accommodated the F-117s on a taxi-through basis, linking from and to the extensive network of taxiways. This aircraft carries mission markings below the cockpit *(Ian Macfadyen)*

Loaded with 2000 lb laser
guided bombs, this F-15E Strike Eagle
is ready for action at Al Kharji.
Equipped with the Low Altitude
Navigation and Targeting Infrared
System for Night (LANTIRN),
the F-15E's operational debut was
very successful *(Randy Jolly)*

Above and opposite A pair of F-15Es heavily laden with cluster bombs and long-range fuel tanks take off from Al Kharji. These dark-grey painted Strike Eagles are from the 336th TFS, which was the first unit to become operational on the type at Seymour Johnson AFB in 1989 *(Randy Jolly)*

A total of 18 EF-111A Ravens was deployed from the 366th TFW, Mountain Home AFB, Idaho, to Al Tauf AB, Saudi Arabia, in November 1990 to operate with 66 F-111Fs from the 48th TFW, normally based at RAF Lakenheath. They retained their normal two-tone grey colour scheme. By the end of operations most aircraft carried toned down mission markings on the port side of the fuselage below their cockpits *(Randy Jolly)*

Above Another 355th TFS A-10A (78-0591) was adorned as 'Kelly Marie's Secrit Weapin' as a winged bomb *(David F Brown)*

Left Flown to King Fahd Air Base, Saudi Arabia, on 15 August 1990 to join the 354th TFW (P), this A-10A Thunderbolt II (78-0654) was from the 355th TFS at Myrtle Beach, South Carolina. Retaining its green camouflage, this aircraft has individual nose art *(David F Brown)*

Above Thunderbolt 79-0158 was decorated as 'Falcon 1', also coming from Myrtle Beach's 355th *(David F Brown)*

Right On return to Alconbury from Saudi Arabia the A-10As displayed a vast range of mission markings. 'Freedom War-Hog' included 58 bombs, 4 radar units, 1 Scud launcher, 12 artillery pieces, 14 tanks, 8 armoured cars and 17 lorries *(Tony Holmes)*

Opposite The 354th TFW(P), which comprised a total of 144 A-10As, also included elements from the 23rd TFW at England AFB, Louisiana, the 925th TFG at New Orleans, Louisiana, the 602nd TACW at Davis-Monthan, Arizona, and the 10th TFW at RAF Alconbury. 'Freedom War-Hog' shown here came from the UK airfield, where it is operated by the 511th TFS of the 10th TFW *(Tony Holmes)*

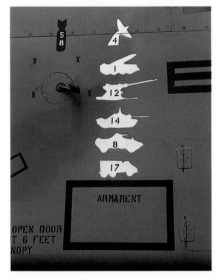

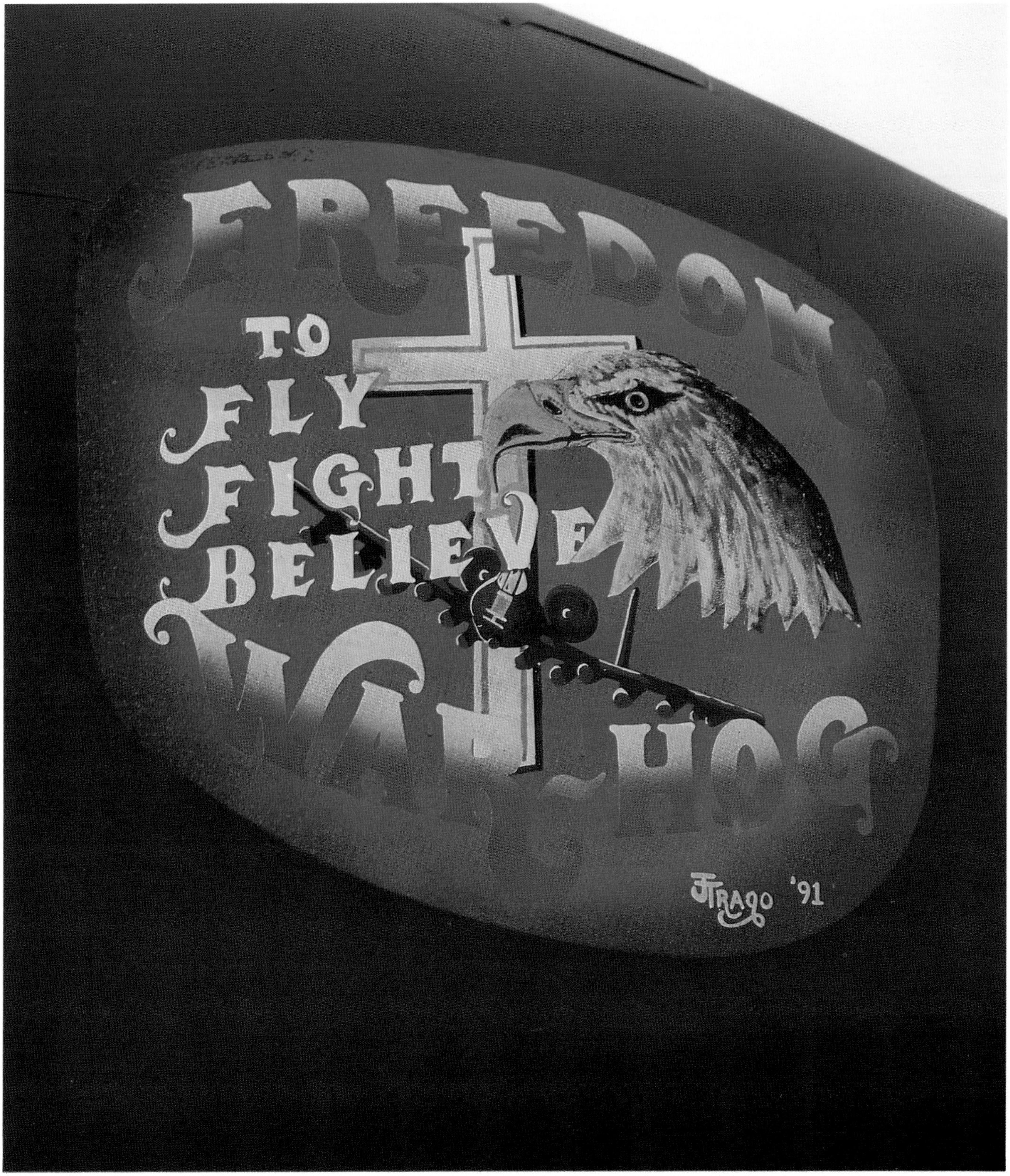
FREEDOM
TO
FLY
FIGHT
BELIEVE
JTRAGO '91

Above Of the 44 Iraqi aircraft believed shot down during and immediately after the Gulf War no fewer than 37 were destroyed by USAF F-15C Eagles. This aircraft, 85-0102 from the 58th TFS/33rd TFW based at Eglin, Florida, and operated from Tabuk, Saudi Arabia, downed three Iraqis, as recorded on the side of the Eagle. On 29 January 1991 Captain D G Rose shot down a MiG-23 using an AIM-7 Sparrow and on 7 February Captain A R Murphy is credited with two Sukhoi Su-22s, again firing AIM-7s. The nose art shows the appropriate name 'Gulf Spirit' *(David F Brown)*

Above right Another successful F-15C Eagle from the same unit, 85–0114 provides more detail of its two 'kills' – a MiG-29 on 19 January, which crashed after pursuit by Captain Cesar Rodriguez, and a MiG-23 shot down using an AIM-7 missile on 26 January by the same pilot. The 33rd TFW(P) was based at Tabuk alongside the RAF strike Tornado GR.1s from October 1990, providing air defence *(David F Brown)*

Right The 33rd TFW's Operation *Desert Storm* tally board attached to their Eglin hangar door – '33rd TFW 16 – Iraq 0'; 16 Iraqi aircraft destroyed with no Eagles lost *(David F Brown)*

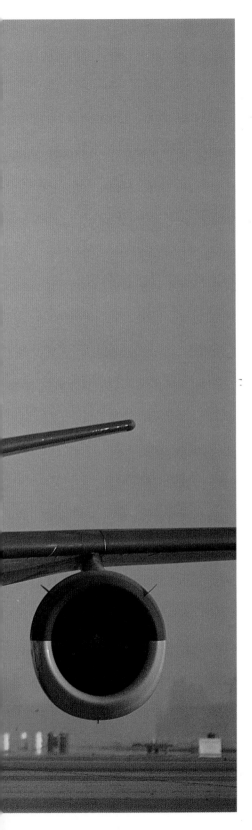

Above KC-135s from most Strategic Air Command refuelling squadrons, Air National Guard and Air Force Reserve units were deployed to Europe or the Middle East during the war, operating from RAF Mildenhall, RAF Alconbury, RAF Upper Heyford, Akrotiri (Cyprus), Mont-de-Marsan (France), Avord (France), Zaragoza (Spain), Sigonella (Sicily), Incirlik (Turkey), Sharjah, Qatar, Masirah, Seeb, Bahrain, Dhahran, King Kahlid International and Riyadh Military City. This KC-135R (10300) of the 340th AREFW is refuelling a C-5A Galaxy of the 443rd MAW en route to the Gulf *(Randy Jolly)*

Left Air-to-air refuelling was an essential feature of Operation *Desert Storm* for most combat aircraft operating over Iraq and for deployments and long-range non-stop missions from outside the Gulf region. This KC-10A 'Swamp Rat' from the 2nd BMW, Barksdale AFB, Louisiana, was one of 46 Extenders deployed to CENTCOM *(Randy Jolly)*

Above A total of 86 B-52Gs was allocated in support of *Desert Storm*, with 64 actually deployed to CENTCOM. The 806th BMW(P) was established at RAF Fairford on 5 February, the 801st BMW(P) at Moron (Spain), the 4300th BMW(P) at Diego Garcia (Indian Ocean) and the 1708th BMW(P) at Jeddah (Saudi Arabia) having all been set up earlier. This Stratofortress (80218) is from the 69th BS/42nd BMW Loring AFB, Maine *(David F Brown)*

Right Nose art and mission markings were carried by most B-52Gs, although some of the more colourful pre-existing designs were toned down or painted over during the war period. This aircraft (80165) from the 416th BMW, Griffiss AFB, New York, is named 'Rolling Thunder' and has a bomb score of 24 *(Walter Wright)*

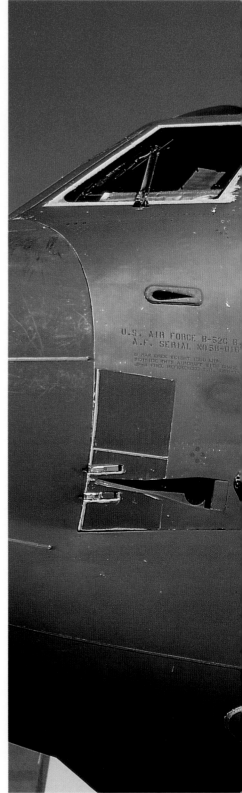

Above The eight B-52Gs of the 806th BMW(P) flew 60 bombing missions from RAF Fairford over Iraq and Kuwait between 9 February and 28 February, dropping 1158 tons of munitions. Two of the aircraft are shown here at the UK base *(Jeremy Flack/API)*

Left Another mission marked B-52G, 0181 from the 2nd BMW, Barksdale AFB, with 20 bombs and showing a witch with a bomb in hand, operating with the 1708th BMW(P) at Jeddah *(Randy Jolly)*

Not only the aircraft received inscriptions. Many of the munitions dropped had messages scrawled on them, usually provided by ground crew. There is no mistaking where this B-52G (80181) 'What's up Doc?' was operating from, with references to England and 'The Fairford Kennel Club' carried on the 2000 lb bombs *(Jeremy Flack/API)*

US Navy and Marine Corps

Left One of eight USN aircraft carriers assigned to Operations *Desert Shield* and *Desert Storm*, the USS *John F Kennedy* (CV-67) had its Carrier Air Wing (CVW-3), tail code AC, active from the Red Sea during the war. Amongst CVW-3's 86 aircraft was this A-6E Intruder (BuNo 162194) from VA-75 'Sunday Punchers' based at NAS Oceana, Virginia. In keeping with other USN aircraft it retained its normal toned down colour scheme and markings, and records 34 missions on its nose. VA-75's aircrew flew more than 3000 hours during 1400 sorties in support of *Desert Shield*, this rigorous flying programme preparing them well for hostilities after 17 January. Participating in strikes deep into Iraq right from the word go, the squadron dropped more than 800 tons of ordnance on the enemy, ranging from 500 lb iron bombs to SLAM rounds *(David F Brown)*

Below Like the *Kennedy*, the USS *Saratoga* (CV-60) operated from the Red Sea with its Carrier Air Wing (CVW-17), tail code AA. This A-6E Intruder (BuNo 159314), flown by Lt J N Zaun, was from VA-35 'Black Panthers' at NAS Oceana, where it was photographed upon the squadron's return in May 1991. This A-6 was in fact Zaun's replacement mount as he had earlier lost his original Intruder during a sortie over Iraq on the opening day of the conflict. Zaun, and his pilot Lt Robert Wetzel, were both captured and interned in a military prison in Baghdad with other coalition POWs until the war ended *(David F Brown)*

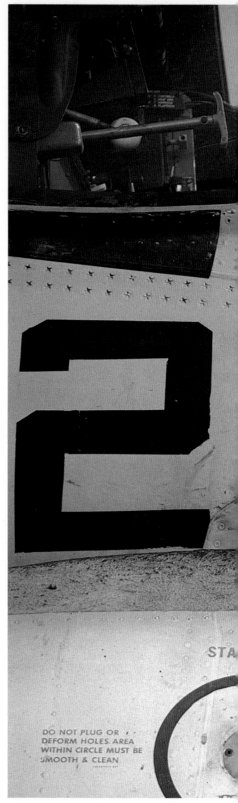

Above A-6E Intruder (BuNo 155678) from VA-85 'Black Falcons' returning home in April 1991 to Oceana, with the cockpit open and a flag flying. It had operated with Carrier Air Wing 1 (CVW-1) on board the USS *America* (CV-66) *(David F Brown)*

Right Another of VA-35's Intruders, KA-6D (BuNo 152606), shows the silhouettes of four FA/18 Hornets and an F-14 Tomcat 'saved' in operations by in-flight refuelling, together with the pilot's name, Lt D L Dixon, below the cockpit on the port side *(David F Brown)*

Above Now totally replaced by the F/A-18, the A-7E Corsair II was deployed aboard the *John F Kennedy* for what will undoubtedly be the type's final operational deployment. Operating as part CVW-3, the Corsair IIs (24 in total) came from VA-72 'Blue Hawks' and VA-46 Clansman, based at Cecil Field, Florida. This A-7E (BuNo 160552/Modex 400/AC) of VA-72 was painted in a two-tone desert brown scheme instead of the standard grey overall and displayed 33 'camel' emblems on the nose, representing missions flown *(David F Brown)*

Left The US Marine Corps carried more nose art and mission markings on its aircraft than the US Navy. This A-6E (BuNo 160431) from VMA(AW)-533 'Hawks', based at MCAS Cherry Point, North Carolina, was assigned to the 3rd Marine Air Wing and operated from Shaik Isa Air Base, Bahrain, with Marine Air Group 11, during *Desert Storm*. It carries the name 'Bird Jog' and has 30 bomb mission markings under the cockpit *(David F Brown)*

Above Another example from VA-72 back at its home base at Cecil Field is A-7E (BuNo 160872), coded 414, which also showed evidence of the many operational missions flown. On the first night of *Desert Storm*, the 'Bluehawks' expended no fewer than 21 HARM missiles at Iraqi SAM sites. In total, the unit flew 362 combat missions totalling in excess of 1500 hours. After returning from the Gulf, VA-72 was disestablished on 23 May 1991 *(David F Brown)*

Left Corsair BuNo 158819, flown by squadron boss Cdr J R 'Shooter' Sanders of VA-72, had extensive mission markings, with 39 camel emblems, 24 combat missions and a weapons tally of 64 GP bombs, 105 Rockeyes, 10 HARMs and 3 Walleyes *(David F Brown)*

Previous pages Photographed over the Red Sea, A-6E Intruder BuNo 161106 was also assigned to VA-85 aboard *America* as part of CVW-1, with the code 501/AB. It had nine missions recorded at the time this photograph was taken. Initially, VA-85 was tasked with striking deeply into Iraq from its Red Sea base aboard the *America*. As the war progressed, the carrier sailed out into the Persian Gulf, the squadron turning its attention to the Kuwait Theatre of Operations. In total 750 tons of ordnance was expended during 2000 hours of combat flying by the 'Black Falcons' *(Randy Jolly)*

VS-32

DET-ALPHA

WARN IN
CONTA
ACTUATED
SYSTE
EXPLOSIVE
01-S3AA-

EJ

Left and above Apart from USS *Midway* (CV-41), each of the aircraft carriers in the Gulf included 10 S-3A/B Vikings in their air wing for anti-shipping and patrol duties. The Vikings on the *America* came from VS-32 'Maulers', based at NAS Cecil Field. One of these (BuNo 159765/Modex 705/AB) showed evidence of three successful missions against Iraqi radars and destroyed a *Zhuk* Class gunboat, as is graphically shown in the close-up. The gunboat kill was achieved on 20 February 1991, when this aircraft, commanded by Lt Cdr Bruce 'Baja' Bole, was vectored onto a surface contact in the North Persian Gulf by the cruiser USS *Valley Forge* (CG-50). Flying a high-altitude profile to avoid the AAA threat, Bole and his crew engaged the high-speed target with three Mk 32 500 lb bombs plus, mistakenly, with a buddy refuelling pod! Soon after the attack radar contact was lost with the target, and the S-3B was credited with the kill. On a more peaceful note, the goat emblem symbolizes this aircraft's participation in the squadron's temporary det at Souda Bay on the island of Crete, where, according to one wag, facilities consisted of 'a runway and goats' *(David F Brown)*

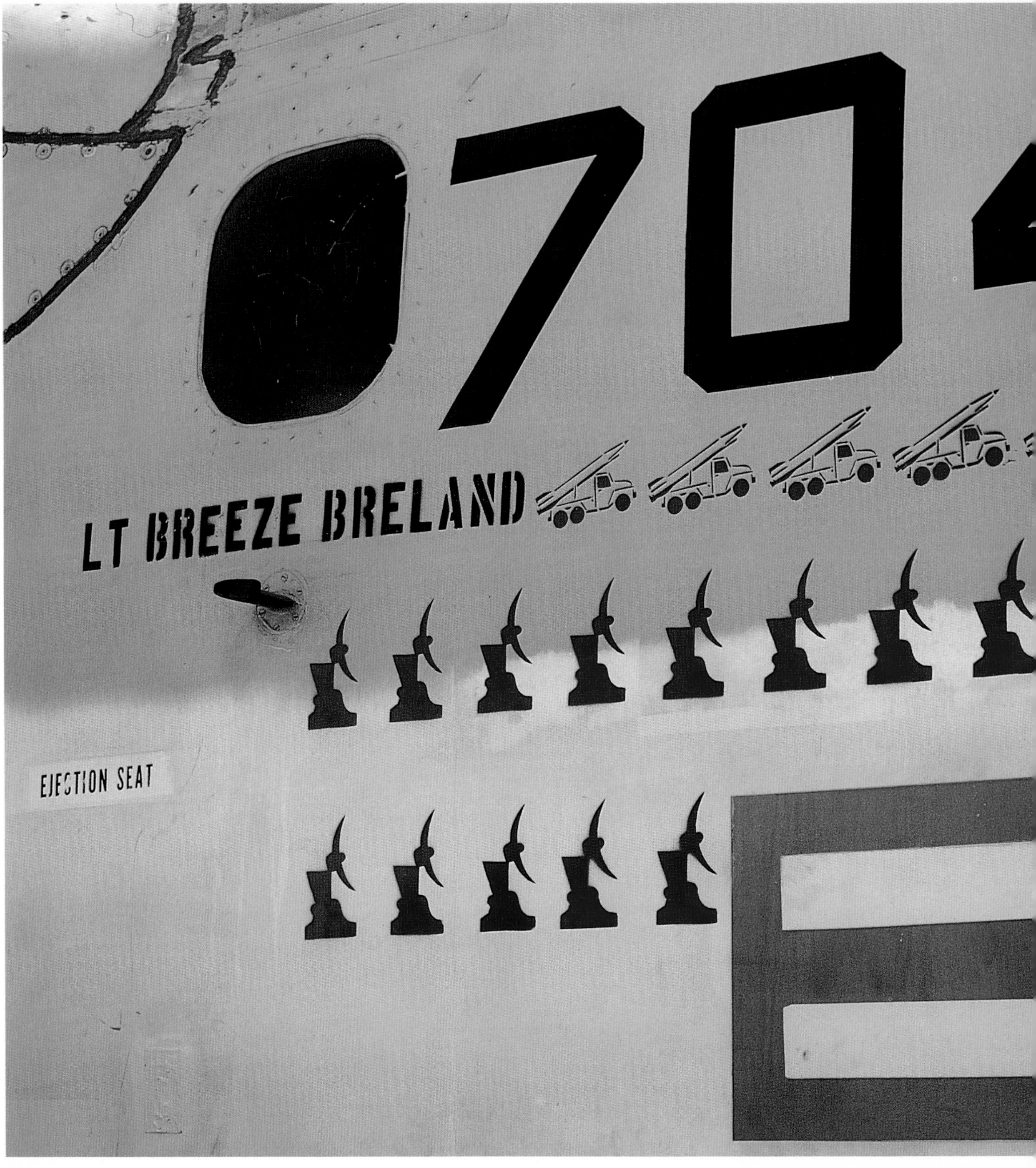

70
LT BREEZE BRELAND
EJECTION SEAT

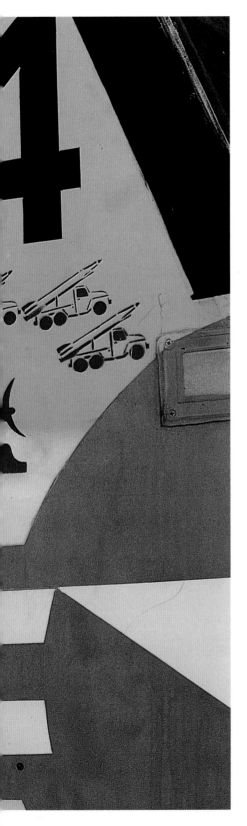

Above Another of the VS-32 S-3B Vikings (BuNo 159751) carries the full title '32nd Torpedo Attack Squadron' and nose art of the 'World Famous Maulers'. The unit achieved a 100 per cent sortie-completion rate throughout the *Desert Storm* cruise *(David F Brown)*

Left Evidence of attacks on seven *Scud* missile launchers and 14 radar installations on S-3B Viking BuNo 159745 (704/AB) of VS-32 are to the credit of Lt 'Breeze' Breland, operating from the *America (David F Brown)*

Above Carrier Air Wing 3 had 24 F-14A Tomcats from VF-32 'Swordsmen' and VF-14 'Tophatters' amongst its 86 operational aircraft. Tomcat BuNo 162694 flown by squadron boss Cdr Bob 'Sundance' Davis ('Gypsy One') and Cdr Tom 'Chain' Zelibar ('Gypsy Two') of VF-32, based at NAS Oceana, had a *Desert Shield* and *Desert Storm* badge painted on it *(David F Brown)*

Left The USS *Theodore Roosevelt* (CVN-71) had 20 F-14As from VF-41 'Black Aces' and VF-84 'Jolly Rogers' operating with its Carrier Air Wing (CVW-8) and wearing the code letters AJ. This aircraft (BuNo 162692) carries the skull and crossbones markings in full colour as the Tomcat is the CO's personal mount *(David F Brown)*

This photograph shows an F-14B, coded 210/NG, of VF-24 'Renegades' from NAS Miramar, California, operating from the USS *Nimitz* (CVN-68), which was the first of three carriers to arrive in the area after the end of the air war. Interestingly, this particular airframe has its air-to-air refuelling probe exposed to the elements, the metal cover which usually shields this apparatus conspicuous by its absence. By participating in this cruise with CVW-9, the 'Renegades' made Pacific fleet history by debuting thisnew version of the Tomcat in the WestPac theatre *(Ian Macfadyen)*

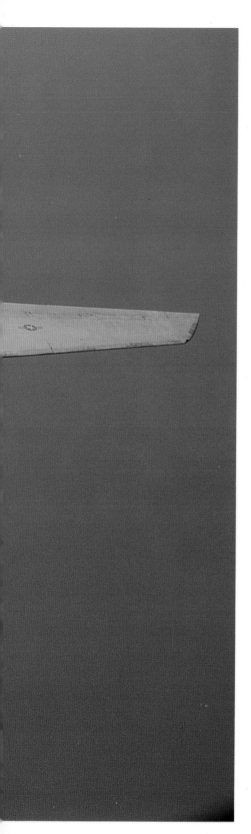

Left, above and overleaf The *America* had 24 F-14A Tomcats from VF-33 'Starfighters' and VF-102 'Diamondbacks' for fighter defence while operating in the Red Sea and Persian Gulf. These air-to-air photographs over the Red Sea show Tomcats from both squadrons. Although the Tomcat units aboard *America* failed to get a score during *Desert Storm*, both squadrons worked tirelessly nevertheless during CAP missions with strike packages en route to Iraq, and later Kuwait. The 'Diamondbacks', for example, logged no fewer than 645 hours in January and 720 hours in February on both CAP and TARPS reconnaissance sorties. CVW-1 was the only air wing to operate in both the eastern and western theatres during *Desert Storm (Randy Jolly)*

Armed with wingtip AIM-9M Sidewinder air-to-air missiles, this F/A-18 Hornet from VFA-82 'Marauders' was heading out on a mission from the *America* when this photograph was taken over the Red Sea. Pilots from VFA-82 remarked that the tanking phase of their five-hour sorties was often more demanding than delivering the ordnance itself. Up to 30 aircraft would queue up behind four KC-135s and await their turn to take fuel, this routine often occuring in darkness. More tanking took place during the trip home. After three weeks of this, the unit sailed with the carrier into the Gulf and commenced cyclic ops on 13 February. This return to a more normal operational profile was made possible by the *America*'s close proximity to Kuwait. By the cessation of hostilities, VFA-82 had delivered more than 1.2 million pounds of ordnance and logged 1309 hours in 597 sorties, all without sustaining any battle damage *(Randy Jolly)*

Above Electronic countermeasures played an important part in the offensive action over Iraq and Kuwait. This EA-6B Prowler from VAQ-137 'Rooks' operating from the *America* is carrying underwing ALQ-99F jammer pods for a key supporting role in a strike mission. Each of the carrier air wings had a quartet of Prowlers on board *(Randy Jolly)*

Above left The second squadron operating F/A-18Cs from the *America* was VFA-86 'Sidewinders', an example of its aircraft (404/AB) in combat fit being shown here, again photographed over the Red Sea *(Randy Jolly)*

Left Two F/A-18C Hornets from VFA/81 'Sunliners' flying from the USS *Saratoga* (CV-60) have the distinction of each shooting down an Iraqi MiG-21 using their AIM-9M Sidewinder air-to-air missiles on the first day of the war. Lt Cdr Mark 'MRT' (Military Rated Thrust) Fox was flying BuNo 163508 and Lt Nick 'Mongo' Mongillo BuNo 163502, shown here. The MiG 'kill' is credited to 'Mongo' on the aircraft's nose. The 'Sunliners' spent eight months at sea during CVW-17's war cruise aboard the 'Super Sara', and aside from achieving the only Navy MiG kills of the war, also suffered the tragic loss of Lt Cdr Michael 'Spike' Speicher on their first strike into Iraq on 17 January *(David F Brown)*

Above Here returned to VAW-124's home base at NAS Norfolk, Virginia, Hawkeye BuNo 161780 taxies in with its wings folded. Again appropriate 'electronic' nose art adorns the E-2C *(David F Brown)*

Left E-2C Hawkeyes provided long-range airborne early warning both for potential attacks on the aircraft carriers and for the movement of Iraqi aircraft towards coalition forces. Each of the US Navy carriers had a squadron of four E-2Cs, while VAW-124 'Zappers' on the *Theodore Roosevelt* had a fifth aircraft. BuNo 161552 from this unit is named 'Miss B Havin', with appropriate nose art *(David F Brown)*

RESCUE

VAW-126

CDR T DUDASH

CO

601

TRANSMITTER PROBE

DO NOT

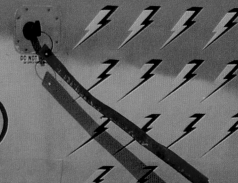

STATIC PORT

60 PSI CARRIER
9 PSI LAND

AN BOYD

Above Providing airborne early warning during the tense days immediately after the cessation of hostilities were the Hawkeyes of VAW-112 'Golden Hawks' based aboard the *Nimitz*. As with the 'new' F-14B, this WestPac marked the operational debut of the upgraded E-2C+, VAW-112 using the aircraft's improved radar and software package to full effect *(Ian Macfadyen)*

Left Carrier Air Wing Three included E-2C Hawkeyes from VAW-126 'Seahawks', this example (BuNo 162616) displaying 14 mission markings on its nose. When Iraq invaded Kuwait in August 1990 the 'Seahawks' had partially deployed to the Panama Canal Zone as part of President Bush's campaign against drugs trafficking. They immediately returned to Norfolk and prepared to sail for the Med. For five and a half months the unit provid AEW cover for the *Kennedy* battlegroup, as well as monitoring key strategic sites in western Saudi Arabia. As the 15 January deadline neared the unit moved closer to the Iraqi frontline and conducted 'sniffer' operations in an effort to collect information on the enemy, and build up a picture of the future battlefield. On station along the border ahead of the first wave in the early hours of 17 January, VAW-126 provided close control for two joint strikes deep into Iraq. Over the next three days the unit flew seven strike support sorties into hostile territory without the loss of a single aircraft under 'Seahawk' control. Over the next seven weeks the unit performed AEW flights over western Saudi Arabia, and more combat strike control and dedicated SAR missions, all of which saw the squadron eventually making a tally of 176 sorties in support of *Desert Storm*. During the cruise, the pilot of this E-2C, squadron boss Cdr Jerry 'Dash' Dudash, passed his 4000-hour mark in Hawkeyes *(David F Brown)*

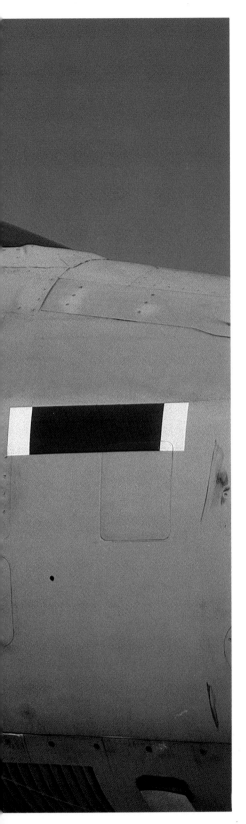

Above By the outbreak of the air war the USMC had 72 Hornets operating from Bahrain, including 24 F/A-18Cs from VFMA-212 'Lancers' and VMFA-232 'Red Devils'*(Randy Jolly)*

Left Four squadrons of USMC F/A-18 Hornets were deployed to Marine Air Group 11 at Shaikh Isa Air Base, Bahrain in August 1990. Amongst these was BuNo 163141 from VMFA-451 'Warlords', based at MCAS Beaufort, which was flown by Capt M A Garrison. The ribbon on the nose denotes that this particular Hornet was hit by a SAM-7 over Kuwait but still returned to base, earning for itself a Purple Heart in the process *(David F Brown)*

CAPT. LINNEKIN

DANGER
EJECTION SEAT & CANOPY
DANGER DANGER

الحرية الكويت

46

Above Another of the 'Ace of Spades' aircraft (BuNo 162944), proclaiming 'Free Kuwait', had a bomb score of 46 *(David F Brown)*

Left Three full squadrons (VMA-231 'Aces', VMA-311 'Tomcats' and VMA-542 'Flying Tigers') of USMC AV-8B Harrier IIs, and a detachment of six aircraft (VMA-513 'Flying Nightmares') were deployed to Sheikh Isa Air Base, Bahrain, in August 1990, moving on to King Abdul Aziz Naval Base, Jubayl (Saudi Arabia) in December. They played a particularly important part in the land war, with forward air control coming from co-located OV-10 Broncos from VMO-1. This aircraft from VMA-231 is based at MCAS Cherry Point, North Carolina. It carries a bomb score of 54 and has rudimentary shark's teeth on its nose *(David F Brown)*

Overleaf Lined up back at Cherry Point, AV-8B BuNo 162943 shows 55 bombs to its credit. VMA-231 lost one of its AV-8Bs (BuNo 162081) in action on 9 February, its pilot, Capt Russel A C Sanborn, being captured. Four further Harriers from other units (BuNo 163518/VMA-311, BuNos 161573 and 163190 both VMA-542, and BuNo 162740/VMA-331) were lost in action *(David F Brown)*

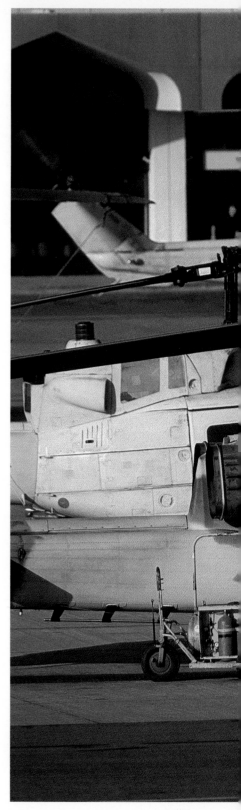

Above On a practice mission over Eastern Saudi Arabia, this AH-1W Super Cobra of HMLA-369 carries a full missile load ready for action against land or sea targets in support of ground forces. As with HMLA-367, this unit was assigned to MAG-16 throughout the conflict *(Randy Jolly)*

Right USMC and US Army helicopters were operated from forward locations in association with the coalition ground forces. Although many started their stay in the Gulf at Al Jubayl, returning there for shipment back to their home bases, they had 'no fixed address' during the period from December to March. These sand-painted AH-1W Super Cobras with Marine Air Group 16 belong to HMLA-367 'Scarface', home based at Camp Pendleton, California *(Randy Jolly)*

US Army

Below and right US Army AH-64 Apache operated by the 82nd Airborne Division at a desert airstrip in northern Saudi Arabia makes a quick refuelling stop while on a combat mission. As can be clearly seen here, the Army broke its long standing tradition of not personalizing their aircraft by allowing the odd set of 'gnashers' to appear on several Apaches in-theatre *(Yves Debay)*

Below right Not all AH-64 crews embraced the new found freedoms regarding nose art however, this Apache looking about as drab as it could possibly be. Mounted under the stub wings is a 19-shot FFAR (folding-fin aircraft rocket) tube, a venerable weapon which again proved its worth in the Gulf *(Yves Debay)*

Above Tactical transport was provided by a large number of US Army UH-60A Black Hawk helicopters. This trio from the 82nd Airborne Division are seen operating over the desert in preparation for *Desert Storm*'s ground phase. A total of more than 6000 hours was flown by the UH-60s *(Yves Debay)*

Right The UH-60As also had a vital role to play as medical evacuation helicopters from frontline field hospitals back to the main medical resources. This Black Hawk, wearing traditional red crosses, was operated by the 101st Air Mobile, and is seen making a running refuelling at a forward desert location *(Yves Debay)*

Above Communications aircraft like this US Army Beech RU-21B were amongst the first fixed-wing types to land at Kuwait Airport after the Iraqis had been driven out. Many of the 'Utes' sported nose art like 0-12087 'Sportsman', photographed in the grey smoke-filled skies of Kuwait City soon after hostilities ceased *(Jeremy Flack/API)*

Above left Early on 24 February over 300 US Army helicopters streamed 45 miles into Iraq to secure a forward operating area. Included in this armada of AH-1s and AH-64s were these UH-1H Hueys from the US Army's 101st Airborne Division, the 'Screaming Eagles' *(Yves Debay)*

Left Once the area had been taken, 118 CH-47 Chinooks, like this one illustrated, and UH-60 Black Hawks of the 101st ferried in 2000 troops and supplies. The twin rotor CH-47s brought in huge quantities of fuel in underslung rubber bladder fuel bags. More troops and weapons followed in over 700 trucks. The huge Cobra base was an essential forward staging area for the 101st AD's successful attacks against Iraqi forces *(Yves Debay)*

RAF

Right The RAF deployed three squadrons of Tornado GR.1s to the Gulf as part of *Operation Granby*. All aircraft were painted in temporary desert pink camouflage (ARTF) and had radar absorbent material (RAM) painted on the leading edges of the wing and tail, intake ducts and pylons. This aircraft, which carries extra large 2250L fuel tanks, was based at Muharraq, Bahrain *(Ian Macfadyen)*

Below A trio of Tornado GR.1s over Bahrain. Most of the RAF aircraft received large, colourful nose art and details of missions flown. ZA471(E) in this formation was named 'Emma', with two JP233, 12 free-fall bomb and 21 laser-guided bomb mission markings *(Ian Macfadyen)*

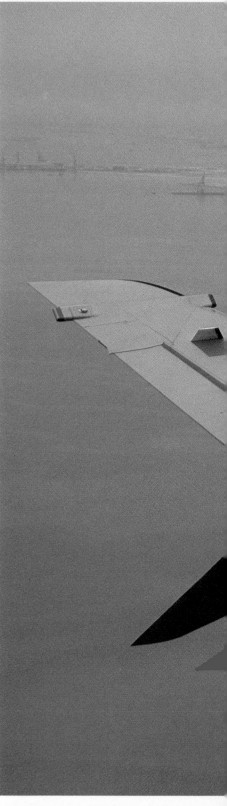

Above Although action in the Gulf could not knock down this Tornado, government cutbacks enforced soon after its return to the UK took a severe toll on its parent unit, No 15 Sqn, based at Laarbruch in Germany. Bombed up, and equipped with outsized 'Hindenburg' external tanks borrowed from the F.3 community, 'FE' heads for the Holbeach range in East Anglia, after returning from active duty *(Ian Black)*

Right Muharraq airfield at Bahrain was for many years until 1971 an important RAF base, a role that returned from late August 1990 when Tornado GR.1s moved in. These were followed by Jaguars, Buccaneers and Victor tankers. Tornado ZD809 'Awesome Annie', a veteran of 33 missions, is seen over what is now Bahrain International Airport *(Ian Macfadyen)*

Above Another of the Muharraq-based Tornado GR.1s (ZA491) showing the carefully painted nose art depicting 'Nikki' and the bomb tally (16 free fall and 13 laser guided bombs) *(Peter R March)*

Left In addition to nose art and mission markings, many of the Tornados carried inscriptions on their munitions before they were delivered to their targets – 'To Saddam – Love Jane' carried on ZA455(J) 'Triffid Airways' for one of its 22 missions. Some GR.1s also carried the names of the ground crew who maintained the aircraft *(Ian Macfadyen)*

Above A number of the Bahrain-based Tornado GR.1s carried the name 'Snoopy Airways', with the cartoon character riding on an LGB painted on the starboard side of the fuselage below the cockpit *(Mike Rondot)*

Above left 'Helen' on Tornado GR.1 ZD892(BJ), photographed during the air war at Bahrain. This particular GR.1 later starred in a BBC news report on a joint Tornado/Buccaneer LGB sortie which was screened across the globe *(Mike Rondot)*

Left 'Gorebusters 91' on Tornado ZD851 (AJ) indicates that 'Amanda Jane' was one of the GR.1s that used the BAe Air Launched Anti-Radar Missile (ALARM) from Tabuk (Saudi Arabia). The weapons tally shows that it fired 11 ALARM, 11 1000 lb bombs and 12 laser guided bombs. It is also known to have dropped at least one JP233 runway denial weapon *(Peter R March)*

Photographed at Muharraq on 8 February, Tornado GR.1 ZD717(CD) had 16 bombs on its tally and carried the titles 'Hello Kuwait – G'bye Iraq' and the Gulf Air insignia. The latter was removed soon afterwards at the request of the airline, who are based at Bahrain. ZD717 was shot down by two Iraqi SA-2 missiles while at medium altitude attacking Al Taqaddum airfield 12 miles west of Falloujah on 14 February. The pilot ejected and was captured; the navigator was killed *(Mike Rondot)*

Several of the Tabuk-based GR.1s were painted with 'sharkmouth' markings like 'MiG Eater' (ZA447 EA) shown here which also has a shark devouring a MiG-29. This is explained by the MiG-29 drawn on the mission tally, the Iraqi fighter having been destroyed on the ground in a raid. It also shows three JP233s, 23 1000 lb bombs and 14 LGBs *(Peter R March)*

Above Four Tornado GR.1s (ZA393, ZD739, ZD844 and ZD848) were modified at Honington and flown to Tabuk on 6 February to use GEC-Marconi's TIALD (Thermal Imaging and Laser Designation) pod, that had hastily been brought to operational standards for No 13 Squadron. A fifth aircraft (ZA406) arrived on 20 February. 'Armoured Charmer' (ZD739) completed 36 missions (31 successfully), designating targets for attendant Tornados *(Peter Cooper)*

Left 'Anola Kay!' (ZD748) was one of nine Tabuk-based Tornado GR.1s equipped to fire BAe ALARM missiles against Iraqi radar. It fired eight ALARMs, as well as one JP233, six free fall and three laser guided bombs during the conflict *(Ian Macfadyen)*

Above Even the two TIALD pods received attention from the Gulf artists. This one being decorated with 'Sandra' from the 'Viz' comic strip the 'Fat Slags' *(Mike Rondot)*

Above left Tornado GR.1 ZD745 (BM) 'Black Magic' on return to Bruggen, its home base, from Dhahran, where it had been operating with No 31 Squadron, had 38 palm trees marked below the cockpit. Tornados at this Saudi base showed their mission tally in this way, without providing details of the munitions dropped *(Andrew March)*

Left A further example of nose artistry at Tabuk – ZA473 'Foxy Mama' with sharkmouth markings and a weapons tally which included three Hunting JP233 runway denial munitions *(Ian Black)*

Above Twelve Buccaneer S.2Bs from Nos 12 and 208 Squadrons at Lossiemouth were flown to Bahrain to provide laser designation for Tornados tasked with precision bombing attacks on specific Iraqi targets from medium level. All aircraft were painted desert pink before departure and carried individual code letters in white on their fins. Although most of the Buccaneers carried a white skull and crossbones on a black flag and the title 'Sky Pirates' on the port side of the nose below their cockpits, this aircraft (XX899 P) had the nose art 'Laser Lips Laura' in its place *(Military Aviation Photographs)*

Right In keeping with other 'graffiti', the various munitions had a colourful variety of inscriptions, including this cryptic message, 'To Saddam. Up Yours! Love Winfields', on this 1000 lb bomb, fitted with a CPU-123B Paveway guidance head and fin, under the wing of a Buccaneer S.2B *(Dave Bolsover)*

Above and right Most of the Buccaneers had very colourful and elaborate nose art together with a name and a very clear bomb tally. 'Sea Witch'/ 'Debbie' appeared on the starboard side of XV863(S) with four black LGBs and two red LGBs. The significance of the colour is the black bombs were dropped by Tornados designated by the Buccaneers, Pave Spike laser designator, and the red bombs were dropped by the Buccaneer itself *(Ian Black)*

Above XW533 'Miss Jolly Roger'/'Fiona'(A) was clearly the 'Sky Pirates' lead aircraft. It achieved 10 LGB designation missions from the 218 flown between 2–27 Feburary *(Peter R March)*

Left Two of the Buccaneers managed to destroy a pair of Iraqi Antonov An-12s at Shayka Mayhar airfield on 27 February, hence the red An-12 silhouette on 'Hello Sailor'/'Caroline' (XX885 L). In addition to the nose art and mission markings, the Buccaneers were each 'branded' with a Scotch Whisky manufacturers' name. This aircraft carried the title 'Famous Grouse' *(Peter R March)*

Above One of the finer pieces of artistry appeared on Jaguar XZ364 which portrayed the Iraqi president receiving a British boot *(Mike Rondot)*

Above left One of the first RAF elements to fly into the Gulf region were 12 Jaguar GR.1As from RAF Coltishall on 11 August 1990. The desert pink painted aircraft were initially based at Thumrait, Oman, but moved to Muharraq, Bahrain, in October. Modified aircraft like this example, XZ356, with up-rated engines, Sky Guardian radar warning receivers and overwing rails to carry AIM-9 Sidewinder air-to-air missiles, were flown out in November. Standard configuration was a centreline fuel tank, four underwing 1000 lb bombs, a Westinghouse ECM pod (port outer pylon) and a Phimat chaff dispenser (on the starboard outer) with overwing Sidewinders. Alternative munitions carried included CBU-87 Rockeye II cluster bombs and CRV-7 2.75 in rockets *(Mike Rondot)*

Left The Jaguars all carried nose art on a more modest scale than the Tornados. 'White Rose' (XZ367) was at first painted as 'Debbie' by the groundcrew, but the pilot had the lady in stockings and underwear replaced *(Mike Rondot)*

Above 'The Guardian reader' (XZ375) was the usual mount of Sqn Ldr Mike Rondot, which shows 17 bombing missions forward of the engine intake. On this occasion he was flying another aircraft in order to take this photograph *(Mike Rondot)*

Left Air-to-air refuelling by VC10s of No 101 Squadron and Victor K.2s of No 55 Squadron was an essential ingredient of operational missions over Iraq by Jaguars and Tornados. Here VC10K2 ZA144 refuels a pair of fully armed Jaguars heading for a target north of the border. The VC10s were based at King Khalid International Airport (KKIA), Riyadh, during the war period *(Mike Rondot)*

Above Although Victor K.2s were involved in 'trailing' Jaguars and Tornados to and from the Gulf, it was not until mid-December that they were based permanently at Muharraq, with the initial task of refuelling the co-located Jaguars. Here XM715 is topping up a Jaguar GR.1A from its right wing drogue. The tankers remained in their appropriate hemp-coloured paint scheme throught the conflict *(Mike Rondot)*

Above left The rare sight of all nine of No 101 Squadron's VC10 K2/K3s lined up on the apron at KKIA on 21 January between sorties *(Ian Macfadyen)*

Left The VC10s received standard nose markings in the form of BP colours and 'The Empire Strikes Back'. After returning from the Gulf some aircraft, like this K.3 ZA148(G), also received mission symbols (46) to represent the number of operational refuelling sorties flown *(Tony Holmes)*

Sweet Sue

All but one of the Victor K.2s had large female figures all carrying spears painted below their cockpits on the port side of the fuselage – XH671 'Sweet Sue' (originally 'Slinky Sue') and XM717 'Lucky Lou' are shown here *(Peter R March)*

Above The finished article. A resplendent 'Teasin Tina' adorns the nose of XM715 *(Dave Bolsover)*

Left XM715 'Teasin Tina' is partly completed, with just the flesh painted into the outline – the artist's 'model' is at hand for reference *(Ian Macfadyen)*

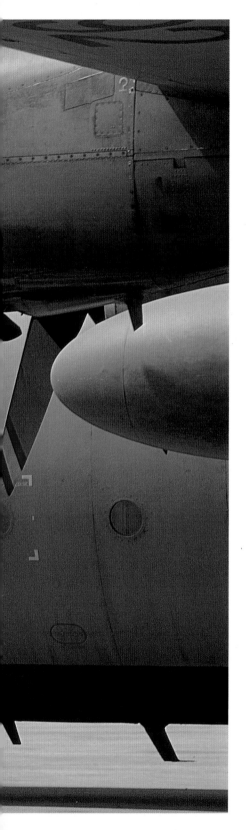

Above Two Tristar KC.1s, ZD949 and ZD951, from No 216 Squadron at RAF Brize Norton were based at KKIA, Riyadh, during the war period operating alongside the VC10s to provide AAR for the Tornado GR.1s and F.3s. Their shiny white and silver scheme was given a coat of desert pink alkali removable temporary finish (ARTF) by Marshalls of Cambridge in mid-January. This earned them the nickname 'Pink Pigs', with ZD949 dubbed 'Pinky' and ZD951 (shown here) 'Perky' *(Peter R March)*

Left Lyneham's Hercules Wing was extremely busy from early August providing essential transport links with the Gulf for all three services. The RAF Air Transport Detachment was set up at KKIA, Riyadh, on 30 October 1990 to provide in-theatre transport. By mid-January it had seven RAF Hercules and a pair from the RNZAF on strength. At least two additional Hercules were painted all over desert pink (a lighter shade than the Tristars). Most of the aircraft based at KKIA acquired nose art, including 'Denis the Menace' on XV292, photographed at Qaisumah in northern Saudi Arabia, one of the regular calling points *(Peter R March)*

Above A detachment of Nimrod MR.2Ps was maintained at Seeb, Oman, from mid-August 1990. Initially from No 120 Squadron, they were later joined by crews and aircraft from No 206 Squadron (Kinloss) and No 42 Squadron (St Mawgan). The Nimrods were given some attention before departure and were fitted to carry the BOZ-107 chaff/flare pod and self defence AIM-9 Sidewinders if necessary. At least two of the aircraft carried large nose art – XV235 'Muscat Belle' (shown here) and XV258 'Guernsey's Girl', whilst one of No 42's had detailed mission markings and the emblem 'Battle Star 42' *(John Meston)*

Above right The RAF sent more than two dozen Puma HC.1s from Nos 33 and 230 Squadrons to the Gulf for the Support Helicopter Force. They were painted in desert pink camouflage overall and had numerous operational modifications including infrared jammers and radar warning receivers. From early in the air war the Pumas were given white 'invasion' stripes around the rear fuselage to aid identification. XW224(S) is seen here at rest in a desert location *(Stuart Black)*

Right On their return to the UK the hard worked Pumas looked very much worse for wear with areas of the pink ARTF already worn off by the harsh environment in which they had been working *(Brian S Strickland)*

Above A total of 17 Chinook HC.1s from Nos 7 and 18 Squadrons and No 240 OCU were operational in Saudi Arabia by mid-January. Some of the Chinooks (as this example ZA707) were given differing pink and black camouflage patterns for night operations *(Brian S Strickland)*

Right Chinook HC.1 ZA713 was fitted with special equipment including engine sand filters, a NAVSTAR Global Positioning System, improved communications, radar warning receivers, plus chaff and flare dispensers. This example could also carry a 7.62 mm machine gun in the forward door, for which a cartridge ejector tube was provided *(Patrick Allen)*

Royal Navy and Army Air Corps

Royal Navy Lynx HAS.3s armed with Sea Skua missiles destroyed 15 Iraqi naval vessels and flew over 250 sorties from *Gloucester, Cardiff, London, Manchester* and *Brazen*. They retained their normal sea grey colour scheme but carried a large union flag on the rear of the fuselage door, as on ZD253 (342) *(Ian Macfadyen)*

Above HMS *Cardiff*'s busy Lynx HAS.3 claimed the destruction of six Iraqi vessels by Sea Skua missiles according to the nose mission markings. The first of these, a *Zhuk* class patrol boat, was attacked at night, the Lynx crew being assisted by a Nimrod and HMS *London*'s Lynx *(Brian S Strickland)*

Left HMS *London*'s Lynx HAS.3 XZ227 (405) taking off from the parent ship. It is carrying *Yellow Veil* jamming equipment and a *Sandpiper* thermal imaging system *(Patrick Allen)*

Three squadrons of Sea King HC.4s were deployed to the Gulf to join the Support Helicopter Force. Yeovilton-based No 846 Naval Air Squadron (NAS) was the first to be sent, followed by No 847 NAS and the specially commissioned No 848 NAS early in January 1991. They provided support for the 1st Armoured Division alongside the RAF Pumas and Chinooks and were additionally tasked to operate from the Primary Casualty Receiving Ship (PCRS) *RFA Argus*. The Sea King HC.4 could accommodate up to nine stretchers and two medical attendants. As illustrated here with the 'V' coded, desert pink painted Sea Kings, No 846 NAS was chosen specifically for this role as most of the crew were experienced in land/desert/sea operations by day or night *(Patrick Allen* and *Jeremy Flack/API)*

Above Although not directly involved in the shooting war, a pair of Defender AL.1s were heavily utilized as staff communication aircraft immediately behind the frontlines. Unlike the Lynxs and Gazelles, the Defenders wore an overall pink paint scheme, the shade of which suggests it came from RAF stocks *(Duncan Cubitt)*

Opposite Army Air Corps helicopters were delivered to the Gulf by sea, arriving at Al Jubayl by the end of December 1990. They comprised anti-tank TOW equipped Lynx AH.7s and reconnaissance Gazelle AH.1s, mainly from No 4 Regiment AAC. Their task was to give anti-tank support to the 1st (British) Armoured Division. The helicopters were painted in a two-tone sand coloured camouflage (rather more 'yellow' than the RAF's 'pink') and carried additional black markings once the land forces went into action. The Lynx AH.7, which was operating in combat in its anti-tank role for the first time, carried sand filters, infrared suppressors for the engine exhausts, radar warning receivers and improved navigational aids. Some of the Lynx were also armed with a 7.62 mm GPMG for additional ground suppression *(Jeremy Flack/API)*

The French and Saudi forces

The French Air Force (*Armée de l'Air Française*) deployed two squadrons of Jaguar As to the Gulf for ground attack duties on a similar basis to the RAF aircraft. They were based at Al Ahsa airfield near Hofuf, Saudi Arabia, during the air war

Above Logistical helicopter support for French Army units came from Pumas of the *Aviation Legère de L'Armée de Terre*. This example, No 164/ADE, here flying low over the desert, has invasion markings applied to the standard sand camouflage. It was based at Hafar Al Bateau *(Yves Debay)*

Above left Dismantled at KKIA ready for shipment back to France, this Jaguar A was damaged by anti-aircraft artillery and suffered an engine fire during the opening strike on Kuwait on 17 January. The cockpit canopy was pierced with bullet holes, but the pilot still managed to get the Jaguar back *(Bob Archer)*

Left The French AF operated its DC-8s from KKIA, Riyadh, for troop andcargo transport in much the same way as the RAF used its VC10 C.1s of No 10 Squadron. An airborne command and control version was also operated during the air war. A DC8-72F is seen here on turn-round at Riyadh *(Peter R March)*

Above A French Army Aviation SA.342M Gazelle, one of a number operated for reconnaissance, and armed with HOT missiles or a 20 mm cannon for anti-tank and armoured vehicle action. Sand camouflage and engine sand filters/IR heat deflectors were fitted to the Gazelles prior to their delivery on board the French Navy aircraft carrier *Clemençeau (Yves Debay)*

Above right Contributing to the massive air-to-air refuelling tasks performed by the coalition tankers in the Gulf were eight KE-3As of No 18 Sqn Royal Saudi AF. Based at Riyadh, the squadron also operates five dedicated AEW
E-3A Sentries *(Ian Macfadyen)*

Right Although both RAF and RSAF Tornado F.3/ADVs were available for patrol duties over Iraq, this task largely fell to RSAF and USAF F-15C Eagles. Here RSAF ADV No 2911 is seen taxying for take-off at Dhahran*(Yves Debay)*

Right RSAF C-130H Hercules were kept busy both in-theatre and on transport flights to and from Cyprus/ Europe. The Hercules sported nose badges and in general became more colourful as the war proceeded (*Yves Debay*)

Below War booty! Captured intact by Marine Corps ground forces pushing through Kuwait, this Bell 214ST was just one of the many souvenirs (albeit a very large one!) brought home by the coalition forces. Originally part of a fleet of over 40 214STs operated by the Iraqi Army, this virtually brand-new Bell now resides at MCAS El Toro in California (*David F Brown*)